LIBRARY
COMMUNITY HIGH SCHOOL
326 Joliet St.
West Chicago, Ill. 60185

DEMC⊘

COUNTDOWN TO SPACE

MARS–
The Fourth Planet

Michael D. Cole

Series Advisors:
Marianne J. Dyson
Former NASA Flight Controller
and
Gregory L. Vogt, Ed. D.
NASA Aerospace Educational Specialist

Enslow Publishers, Inc.

40 Industrial Road	PO Box 38
Box 398	Aldershot
Berkeley Heights, NJ 07922	Hants GU12 6BP
USA	UK

http://www.enslow.com

Library of Congress Cataloging-in-Publication Data

Cole, Michael D.
   Mars—the fourth planet
      p. cm. — (Countdown to space)
   Includes bibliographical references and index.
   Summary: Describes the fourth planet from the sun, including its discovery, terrain, temperature, and characteristics, and examines the possibility of life on the Red Planet.
   ISBN 0-7660-1949-7
   1. Mars (Planet)—Juvenile literature. [1. Mars (Planet)] I. Title. II. Series.
QB641 .C64 2002
523.43—dc21

                                   2001002901

Printed in the United States of America

10 9 8 7 6 5 4 3 2 1

To Our Readers: We have done our best to make sure all Internet Addresses in this book were active and appropriate when we went to press. However, the author and the publisher have no control over and assume no liability for the material available on those Internet sites or on other Web sites they may link to. Any comments or suggestions can be sent by e-mail to comments@enslow.com or to the address on the back cover.

Illustration Credits: AP Photo/Kevork Djansezian, p. 9; © Corel Corporation, p. 13; Phil James (University of Toledo), Todd Clancy (Space Science Institute), Steve Lee (University of Colorado), and NASA, p. 41; JPL/NASA, pp. 4, 6, 8; Lunar and Planetary Institute (LPI), pp. 15, 17, 22; NASA, pp. 12, 19, 29, 30–31, 38; NASA, JPL, Malin Space Science Systems, pp. 21, 27, 35; NASA/LPI, p. 40; NASA/USGS, p. 33; USGS, pp. 24–25.

Cover Illustration: NASA (foreground); Raghvendra Sahai and John Trauger (JPL), the WFPC2 science team, NASA, and AURA/STScI (background).

CONTENTS

The Pathfinder is blasted into space aboard a NASA rocket on December 6, 1996. It arrived at Mars seven months later.

I

Martian Visitor

It was July 4, 1997.

The robotic spacecraft *Pathfinder* drifted down on a parachute toward the dusty red surface of Mars. It had been traveling through space for seven months, and was now ready to make its landing.

At about one hundred feet above the surface, the parachute was released from the spacecraft as planned. The spacecraft continued to drop toward the rocks and dust below. Moments later, *Pathfinder* hit the surface of Mars . . . and bounced!

While drifting down on the parachute, the spacecraft had inflated four large air bags all around it. The air bags were designed to cushion *Pathfinder*'s landing, and allowed the spacecraft to carry a much smaller amount of fuel in its landing rockets.

When the bouncing *Pathfinder* came to rest, the air bags deflated. The spacecraft then settled itself into an upright position on the Martian surface. *Pathfinder*, a spacecraft no larger than a kitchen table, had successfully landed on Mars.[1]

An airbag inflation test is done as part of the preparation for the Pathfinder *mission. The airbags helped the spacecraft to safely land on Mars.*

Seven hours after *Pathfinder* landed, it began sending back pictures of the alien landscape. But scientists had seen pictures of the Martian surface before. Two *Viking* spacecraft had landed on Mars in 1976. This time, however, scientists were ready to make a further exploration of the Red Planet.

Later, *Pathfinder* extended a metal ramp to the surface. Latches released, and a rover with six metal wheels, a solar panel, two cameras, and an antenna slowly rolled down the ramp. The little rover, about the size of a microwave oven, was called *Sojourner*.

One hundred twenty million miles (193 million kilometers) away, on Earth, scientist Brian Cooper drove the rover using computer equipment. Cooper worked at the Jet Propulsion Laboratory (JPL) in Pasadena, California, part of the National Aeronautics and Space Administration (NASA). JPL is the control center for most space probes to other planets. Although Cooper controlled the rover, he could not drive *Sojourner* like a radio-controlled car. The distance between Earth and Mars is too great. When *Sojourner* took a picture of its surroundings, the electronic signal took more than ten minutes to reach Earth. Any command signals that Cooper sent back to the rover took another eleven minutes to reach Mars. In other words, communication between Cooper and the rover took at least twenty-two minutes.

"If I were to see a cliff on my computer screen and tell

The Sojourner *rover rolled out of* Pathfinder *and onto the Red Planet. Its instruments included two cameras to photograph the Martian surface.*

the rover to stop, it would have fallen off by the time my signal got there," Cooper said.[2]

For that reason, all of *Sojourner*'s movements were planned very carefully. *Pathfinder* took pictures of the area surrounding the rover. From these pictures, a list of movements was planned. Cooper then fed the pictures into his computer. Wearing a set of goggles that showed him a three-dimensional view of the area around *Sojourner*, he could change the planned movements into a set of commands for the rover.

"I can see the surface of Mars as if I'm standing

there," he said. "I can see depth. I can see how far away the rocks are."[3]

Cooper's commands were then sent to the *Pathfinder* spacecraft, which relayed them to *Sojourner*. The rover's movements across the surface allowed scientists to investigate different types of Martian rock around *Pathfinder*'s landing site. Its instruments revealed new information about the makeup of the planet's surface. Scientists now had more evidence that water had once existed on the planet, and had played a part in shaping

Wearing 3-D glasses, scientist Brian Cooper controlled the Sojourner rover from a control room at NASA's Jet Propulsion Laboratory in California.

its present landscape. The discoveries shed new light on how and when Mars was formed, and whether life might have existed earlier in the planet's history.

The great distance between Mars and Earth made operating *Sojourner* a delicate process for Cooper and other scientists at JPL. Yet, Mars is one of Earth's closest neighbors in space. Its closeness has made it a place of great curiosity to astronomers and scientists.

Interest in Mars goes back much further than the age of science. The planet's red color and its movements through the night sky have fascinated humans for thousands of years.

2

Angry Red Planet

Mars is one of Earth's nearest neighbors in space. The Moon orbits Earth at an average distance of about 240,000 miles (384,000 kilometers). The next nearest neighbor is the planet Venus, which comes as close as 24 million miles (38 million kilometers) from Earth. After the Moon and Venus, Mars is our next closest neighbor.

Mars passes as close to Earth as 34 million miles (54 million kilometers). But when Mars and Earth are at opposite sides of their orbits around the Sun, the two planets are separated by 249 million miles (400 million kilometers) of space. That distance is nearly eight times farther than when the two planets are closest.

You can see Mars at night. You do not even need binoculars. Mars, as well as Mercury, Venus, Jupiter, and

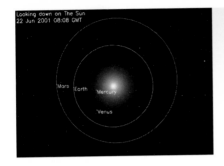

Sometimes Mars and Earth are close to each other during their orbits of the Sun, as shown here. At that point, they are 34 million miles apart.

Saturn, were identified in the night sky by ancient cultures. The planets caught the attention of early astronomers because their movements were unusual compared to the movements of the stars. Our view of the stars changes from month to month as Earth travels in its orbit around the Sun. But the stars appear in the same patterns, or constellations, year after year, century after century. Mars and the other visible planets, however, appear to move through the sky from one area of stars to another. This occurs because the planets are orbiting the Sun. Their movement through space causes them, over periods of months and years, to be seen in different parts of the night sky from Earth. The word *planet* comes from the Greek word meaning "wanderer."

Mars's red color in the night sky was important to ancient myths and beliefs. Early civilizations saw the planet's redness as a symbol of blood and war, and a sign that bad things were to come. The ancient Greeks identified the planet with their god of war, Ares. The Romans later adopted the Greek gods, giving them new names. Ares became Mars, and the planet was given the name of this Roman god of war.[1]

Although we have long known that Mars is not a god or a bringer of war, strange beliefs about Mars continued right into the twentieth century. Telescopes up to that time were not able to show much detail about the surface of Mars. That lack of detail let people imagine what might exist on the neighboring Red Planet.[2]

Mars is named after the Roman god of war.

Early Ideas About Mars

The blurry images of Mars in his telescope led one astronomer, Percival Lowell, to believe that he saw a system of canals crisscrossing the surface of the planet in the late 1890s. Lowell was from a wealthy American family. He had built a large telescope and observatory in Flagstaff, Arizona, to study Mars. His telescope was modern at the time, but only strong enough to see patches of dark and light across the planet's reddish surface. Lowell's enthusiastic imagination turned these blurry patches into a complex system of canals. He believed that intelligent Martian beings had built the canals to carry water from the planet's melting polar ice caps to its drier areas.[3]

Lowell's sensational claims created a public fascination with Mars and the possibility that intelligent beings might live there. His observations were scientific, but his conclusions about what he saw were wrong. Those wrong ideas sparked many people's imaginations. Tales of Martians, alien invasions, and "little green men" have appeared in books, movies, and television programs ever since.

Size and Composition

Mars is the fourth planet from the Sun, after Mercury, Venus, and Earth. It is approximately 4,000 miles (6,800 kilometers) wide, about half the size of Earth. Because so much of Earth is covered by oceans, the amount of land surface on the two planets is nearly equal.

Mars, along with Mercury, Venus, and Earth, is a terrestrial planet. This means that the planet is made of rock. Other planets in our solar system—Jupiter, Saturn, Uranus, and Neptune—are enormous balls of gas, ice, and a smaller amount of rock. They have no solid surface on which a spacecraft could land. The smallest planet, Pluto, is made of rock and ice.

Mars is made up of a crust layer, a mantle layer, and a central core. The planet's core is about 1,000 miles (1,700 kilometers) across, and is probably made mostly of iron and other heavy metals. Scientists think the mantle layer is composed of molten rock. It is about 3,400 miles (5,440 kilometers) thick. The planet's outer

The terrestrial planets are the four planets closest to the Sun: Mercury, Venus, Earth, and Mars. This diagram shows the relative sizes of these planets.

crust layer varies in thickness from about 50 miles (80 kilometers) near the big volcanoes in the south, to 22 miles (35 kilometers) in the northern lowlands.[4]

The makeup of Mars's layers make it far less massive, or heavy, than Earth. Mars has only one tenth the mass of Earth. Because of Mars's smaller size, it has only about one third of Earth's gravity. If you weighed 100 pounds on Earth, you would weigh about 38 pounds on Mars.

The Martian Surface

Two main types of surface appear on Mars. The older surfaces are the heavily cratered highland areas. These are rough, mountainous areas that have been formed by violent meteorite or asteroid impacts over millions of years. Scientists believe this terrain covers almost two thirds of the planet. The younger, smoother areas of Mars are the plains, which were formed by volcanoes spilling hot lava onto the surface. The plains are smooth because lava flowed over the older cratered surface. Less time has passed for impact craters to accumulate on the newer surface. Scientists think that some of the plains on Mars may have been formed by the slow movement of ground ice in the planet's soil over millions of years.[5]

Mars is called the Red Planet because of its colored appearance in the night sky. This appearance results from the reddish dust that covers much of its surface. Most of the rock covering the surface of Mars is rich in iron, which is a metal. Exposure to the Martian air

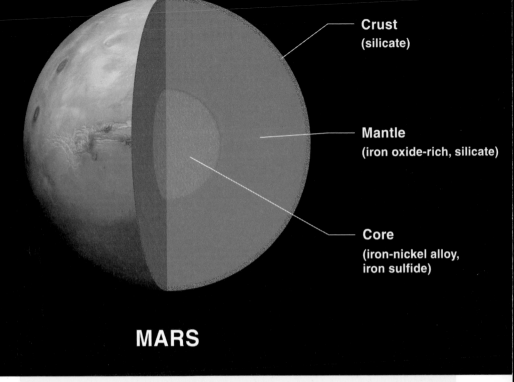

Mars has a crust, mantle, and core.

eventually causes these metallic rocks to undergo oxidation. Quite simply, the surface of Mars is rusting, causing it to appear various shades of red and orange. Those colors can be seen across the millions of miles of space between Mars and Earth.

Mars's Atmosphere

The atmosphere that causes the surface of Mars to rust is much thinner than the atmosphere on Earth. Humans could not breathe on Mars because the thin atmosphere results in a lack of atmospheric pressure. Atmospheric pressure is created by the weight of the atmosphere pressing down. Our lungs, adapted to the atmospheric pressure on Earth, could not pull in the thin air of Mars. The many layers of our atmosphere on Earth cause us to experience a pressure on Earth's surface of 14.7 pounds per square inch. The pressure on the surface of Mars is less than one tenth of a pound per square inch.

No human could survive in the low pressure of Mars. It would cause the oxygen in our blood to form into tiny bubbles that would block our blood vessels and cause death.

The air on Mars is made up mostly of carbon dioxide, nitrogen, and argon, with traces of oxygen, water, and other gases. Wispy clouds of ice form in this atmosphere by evaporating water from the planet's polar ice caps. But these clouds do not last for long. They may produce snow at the polar ice caps, but they never develop into rain clouds or rainstorms.

Enough atmosphere exists, however, to create massive dust storms. Astronomers have observed dust storms on Mars that obscured their view of the planet's entire surface for months. The Hubble Space Telescope, orbiting high above Earth's atmosphere, observed a vast dust storm developing on Mars in the weeks before *Pathfinder* was due to land on the planet. Scientists feared that if the storm spread, it might endanger a successful landing by *Pathfinder*. Luckily the storm died down before the scheduled landing.

Long after such storms are over, the normal winds on

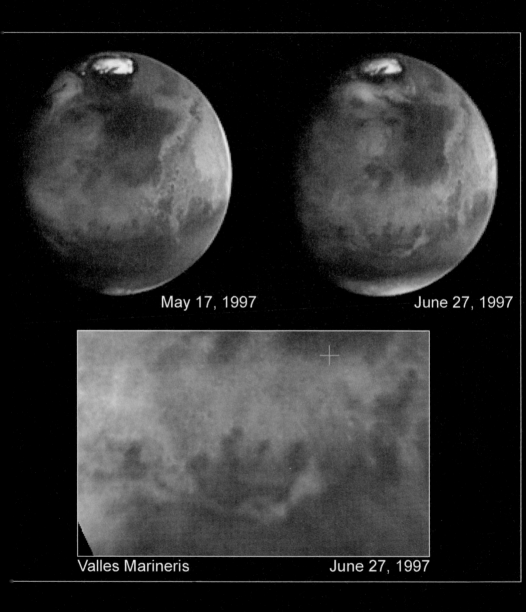

May 17, 1997   June 27, 1997

Valles Marineris   June 27, 1997

On June 27, 1997, the Hubble Space Telescope captured this image of a
dust storm on Mars just weeks before the Pathfinder landing.

Mars continue to blow some of the dust into the air. The constant presence of dust in the air causes the sky above Mars's surface to appear in soft shades of red or pink.

Seasons and Years on Mars

Mars experiences seasons just as Earth does, and for the same reason. Earth is tilted on its axis by 23.5 degrees. During Earth's orbit of the Sun, the hemisphere that is tilted toward the Sun receives more direct sunlight than the hemisphere tilted away from the Sun. This causes our summer and winter seasons. Mars is tilted on its axis 25.1 degrees. This tilt causes seasonal changes in wind and dust storms, and changes in the size of the Martian polar ice caps.[6]

A year on Mars is nearly twice as long as an Earth year. A Martian year is 687 Earth days, while an Earth year is 365 1/4 days. The orbit of Mars is more elliptical, or oval, than Earth's orbit. Because of this, the seasons on Mars last unequal periods of time. On Earth, the four seasons last about the same number of days. But on Mars, the northern hemisphere's spring lasts 199 days, while its autumn lasts only 147 days.

Martian Moons

When the soft red or pink sky of Mars turns dark after sunset, Phobos and Deimos appear. They are the two moons of Mars. Phobos is visible from the planet's surface every night, because it orbits the planet twice a day. Sometimes both moons are present in the night sky,

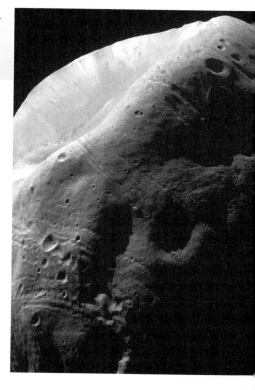

Phobos is the larger of the two moons of Mars. This image shows the largest crater on Phobos.

but Deimos does not appear every night.

Both moons are small and odd-shaped. They are not large enough for gravitational pressure to have shaped them into spheres. Deimos is only twenty miles wide, and Phobos is only slightly larger. Both moons look like enormous boulders in space and are covered with craters. Phobos orbits Mars at a distance closer than any moon orbiting any other planet in the solar system. Its orbit is only 5,813 miles (9,377 kilometers) from the planet's surface. This is less than 3 percent of the distance at which the Moon orbits Earth. Deimos orbits Mars at a distance of nearly 14,000 miles (24,000 kilometers), which is also very close for a moon to orbit a planet.[7]

Temperatures

The orbit of Mars places it an average of 152 million miles (228 million kilometers) from the Sun. That is more than 50 million miles farther from the Sun than

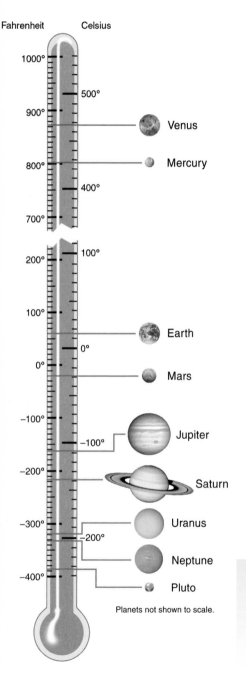

Fahrenheit   Celsius

1000°
              500°
900°   Venus
800°   Mercury
              400°
700°

200°   100°

100°
                        Earth
              0°
0°   Mars

-100°
              -100°   Jupiter

-200°
                        Saturn

-300°   Uranus
              -200°
                        Neptune
-400°
                        Pluto

Planets not shown to scale.

Earth is, resulting in a much colder world. The average temperature on the planet's surface is about -67°F (-5°C). At the planet's equator during summer, spacecraft have recorded temperatures as high as 80°F (27°C). But temperatures at the poles have gone as low as -207°F (-33°C). Between these extremes, the temperature during an average day on Mars is as cold as the coldest temperatures in Antarctica, about -128°F (-90°C).[8]

The planet's lack of water, low temperature, and thin atmosphere, make it difficult or perhaps impossible for life to exist on Mars. However, scientists believe that life may

In general, the surface temperature of the planets decreases with increasing distance from the Sun. Venus is the exception because it has a dense atmosphere that acts as a greenhouse and heats the surface.

have existed on the planet millions of years ago. Some scientists think it is possible that a simple form of microscopic life exists on Mars at or below its surface today. The only sure way to investigate the existence of present life or past life on Mars is to go there.

Mars[9]

Age
About 4 billion years

Diameter
4,212 miles (6,794 kilometers)

Planetary mass
One tenth of Earth's mass (Earth's mass is about 6,000 million, million, million tons)

Distance from Sun
141 million miles
(228 million kilometers)

Distance from Earth
Maximum—248 million miles
(401 million kilometers)
Minimum—34 million miles
(54 million kilometers)

Orbital period (year)
687 Earth days

Rotation period (1 day)
24 hours and 37 minutes

Temperatures
Average of -67° F (-55° C)
Highs at equator—80° F (27° C)
Lows at poles— -207° F (-133° C)

Composition
Core of iron and heavy metals, mantle of probably molten rock, outer crust of solid rock

Atmospheric composition
95 percent carbon dioxide, 2.6 percent nitrogen, 1.6 percent argon, traces of other gases

Wind speeds
Not greater than 60 miles (100 kilometers) per hour

Gravity
38 percent of Earth's gravity

Number of moons
2

Sun's brightness from Mars
44 percent as bright as from Earth

3

Missions to Mars

The first spacecraft to reach Mars was NASA's *Mariner 4* in 1965. *Mariner 4* did not land on Mars, but took pictures and made studies of the planet's atmosphere as it flew by. *Mariner 6* and *Mariner 7* performed similar missions in 1969.

The first United States spacecraft to go into orbit around Mars was *Mariner 9* in 1971. The spacecraft took 7,300 photographs and mapped the entire surface of the planet. *Mariner 9*'s pictures revealed some startling features on the planet's surface.

Images from the spacecraft showed an enormous volcano that scientists named Olympus Mons, after the home of the gods in Greek mythology. Olympus Mons is larger than any volcano or mountain on Earth. In fact, it is the largest known volcano in the solar system. At over 16 miles (26 kilometers) high, its summit is more than twice as high as Mt. Everest, Earth's tallest mountain. The gigantic base of Olympus Mons covers an area the size of the state of Arizona.[1]

Although Olympus Mons is much taller than Mt. Everest, it does not have towering peaks and jagged cliffs. Olympus Mons is shaped like an enormous pancake spread out over a flat plain. It slopes toward the flat volcanic crater at its peak very gradually, not steeply and dramatically like some of the great mountains on Earth.

Mariner 9's mapping images also revealed a vast system of canyons called the Valles Marineris. The canyons stretch across an area near Mars's equator for more than 2,500 miles (4,000 kilometers). The central region of the canyon is more than 370

Olympus Mons is more than twice as tall as Mount Everest and about as wide as the entire chain of Hawaiian islands. This giant volcano is nearly as flat as a pancake.

miles (700 kilometers) wide, and drops down to more than 4 miles (7 kilometers) deep. The canyon system's enormous dimensions dwarf the Earth's Grand Canyon in Arizona. The Valles Marineris is an unmistakable feature cutting across the planet's equator, easily seen by the naked eye from space. It is the largest and deepest canyon known in the solar system. If it existed on Earth it would stretch from California to New York.[2]

The exploration of Mars took a giant leap forward when *Viking 1* successfully landed on the planet on July 20, 1976. For the first time, images from the spacecraft showed people what it looked like to stand on the surface of Mars. The landscape around *Viking 1* was barren, rocky, and red. The lander's robotic scoop dug into the Martian soil and pulled samples into the spacecraft for analysis by scientific instruments. *Viking 1*, and later *Viking 2*, collected this data and relayed it to Earth. But the studies completed by the spacecraft neither proved nor disproved the existence of life on Mars.

Is There Life on Mars?

The possibility of life on Mars grabbed the public's attention again in 1996. Studies on a meteorite that had been found in Antarctica in 1984 led scientists to believe that it was a piece of Mars. This idea was based on the fact that the meteorite had almost the same makeup as the rock scooped up from Mars by the two Viking spacecraft. But how did a piece of Mars get to Earth?

Scientists explained that the piece of Martian rock was probably blown into space when a large asteroid or comet hit Mars about 16 million years ago. The rock then drifted in space for millions of years, until it fell to Earth, onto the icy surface of Antarctica, about 13,000 years ago. By the end of its journey through space and

The Viking spacecraft was the first to land on Mars. It gave the world its first look at what it was like on the surface of the Red Planet.

down through Earth's atmosphere, it was the size of a large potato. But scientists found what appeared to be remains from fossilized microscopic organisms inside the meteorite—possible evidence of ancient life on Mars.

Former NASA Administrator Daniel Goldin announced that the discovery "points to the possibility that a primitive form of microscopic life may have existed on Mars more than three billion years ago." But he cautioned the public not to let their imaginations run wild. "I want everyone to understand that we are not talking about 'little green men,'" Goldin said. "These are extremely small, single-cell structures. . . . The evidence is exciting, even compelling, but not conclusive. It is a discovery that demands further scientific investigation."[3]

Some scientists wondered if the life-forms had gotten onto the meteorite after it landed on Earth. But most of the microscopic evidence was found inside the rock. This suggests that the ancient organisms were in the rock before it landed. Whether the bits of evidence found in the rock are truly microscopic organisms from Mars is still debated today.[4]

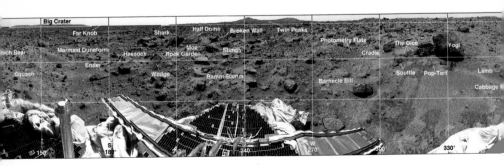

A Volcanic Past

Only months after the announcement about the Mars meteorite, the *Mars Global Surveyor* and *Pathfinder* spacecraft were launched to the Red Planet. *Pathfinder* landed on Mars seven months later, on July 4, 1997, and released the *Sojourner* rover to study the rocks and soil in the area.

Project scientist Brian Cooper and the rest of the team at JPL carefully guided the rover toward a rock. The team named the rock Barnacle Bill because of its barnaclelike appearance. *Sojourner's* instruments analyzed Barnacle Bill and another rock the team named Shark, and found that they were similar to rocks found near volcanoes on Earth. Barnacle Bill and Shark appeared to have melted, hardened, and remelted, suggesting widespread volcanic activity sometime in Mars's past. The rocks also contained evidence that water had existed in the planet's crust more recently than previously thought.[5]

Images from the landing sites around *Viking 1* and *Viking 2* show large rocks spreading toward the horizon in every direction. Scientists believe the large rocks were scattered for many miles

A map of the rocks that were seen at the Mars Pathfinder *landing site includes Barnacle Bill and Shark.*

around the area after the impact of a large meteorite or asteroid. When this object struck Mars, the planet's surface was shattered, and chunks of rock flew into the air. The broken-up rock fell back to the ground around the crater.[6]

Images from the *Pathfinder* landing site also show many stones and rocks, which scientists think were swept into the area by a giant flood in Mars's distant past. Scientists believe that huge discharges of groundwater formed large outflow channels. The sudden rush of water carried the rocks and carved new features on the surface. Gaining new evidence that water helped form some of the surface features on Mars was one of the main scientific achievements of *Pathfinder*.[7]

More Missions

Not all missions to Mars have been successful. The *Mars Climate Orbiter* and *Mars Polar Lander* spacecraft were both lost in 1999. *Mars Climate Orbiter* never entered orbit, and likely crashed into the planet, because of programming errors in the spacecraft's navigation system. *Mars Polar Lander* was lost shortly before it would have landed on the planet. Scientists still do not know what happened to the spacecraft, or why it failed to send back any messages from the surface.

The next spacecraft to arrive successfully at Mars was *Mars Global Surveyor*. The spacecraft spent a full Martian year, 687 Earth days, mapping the planet in great detail. With its original mission completed, the spacecraft continued to send additional images of the Martian surface to scientists at JPL.

Detailed images of some craters and the deep canyons of the Valles Marineris revealed layers that could be sedimentary rock. Sedimentary rock is formed by layers of wet soil being compressed and cemented together over long periods. These rock layers are common on Earth in places where there were once lakes.

"We see distinct, thick layers of rock," said *Mars Global Surveyor* scientist Dr. Michael Malin, "for which a number of lines of evidence indicate that they may have

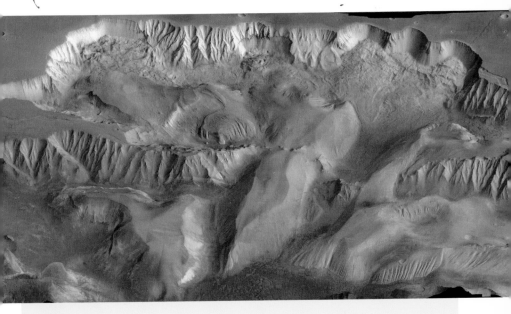

When scientists viewed this image of Valles Marineris on Mars, they saw thick layers of rock. This rock may be sedimentary rock, which is formed by layers of wet soil pressed together over a long time.

33

been formed in lakes or shallow seas." The announcement, which came in December 2000, told of the best evidence yet of a watery Martian past.

"These images," Malin added, "tell us that early Mars was very dynamic and may have been a lot more like Earth than many of us had been thinking."[8]

Other scientists studying the images from *Mars Global Surveyor* agreed.

"Mars seems to continually amaze us with unexpected discoveries," said Dr. Edward Weiler, Associate Administrator for Space Science at NASA. "This finding just might be the key to solving some of the biggest mysteries on Mars."[9]

The sedimentary rock may one day tell scientists about the role water played in the planet's distant past. But *Mars Global Surveyor* also recorded images of gullies that looked like they had been formed recently. These gullies appeared to be created by flowing water and the deposits of soil and rock transported by these flows.

"We think we are seeing evidence of a groundwater supply," Malin said. Dr. Weiler added, "We're no longer talking about a distant time. The debate [about the presence of water on the planet] has moved to present-day Mars."

Malin explained that recently made gullies found on Earth near sources of groundwater look very similar to the gullies discovered on Mars. "They could be a few million years old," he said, "but we cannot rule out that some of them are so recent as to have formed yesterday."[10]

Mars Global Surveyor also made some surprising discoveries at the planet's polar ice caps. Images from the spacecraft showed that the north polar cap has a flat, pitted surface. But images of the southern polar cap showed larger pits, troughs, and flat areas. The frozen southern polar cap looked "like pieces of sliced and broken Swiss cheese," according to Cornell University scientist, Dr. Peter Thomas.

The Newton Crater on Mars has many narrow gullies. Scientists believe they may have been formed by flowing water.

"The unusual shapes of the landforms on the north and south polar caps suggest that these regions have had different climates and histories for thousands or perhaps even millions of years," Thomas said. "The polar images demonstrate again that understanding Mars's complicated history requires studying the many areas in detail, just as understanding the Earth does."[11]

Future Missions

Studying Mars in greater detail means sending more spacecraft there. The *2001 Mars Odyssey* was launched on April 7, 2001. From 2001 to 2004, it will orbit the planet and use its instruments to map the chemical elements and minerals that make up the Martian surface. The spacecraft will be looking for hydrogen, in the form of ice, which may exist just below the surface.

The *2001 Mars Odyssey* will also serve as a communication relay satellite for the Mars exploration rovers that are scheduled to be launched in 2003 or 2004. The two rovers will land at different regions of Mars, and will be able to travel more than a hundred yards per day over the Martian surface. Each rover will be equipped with instruments that will allow it to search for water.

But robotic spacecraft and rovers may not be enough. Human missions to Mars may be required to answer all of our questions about the planet, and finally prove whether life exists or ever existed on Mars. Those first human explorers will be aliens on a world very unlike their own.

4

Mars from Near and Far

The first astronauts on Mars will likely be there for more than just a brief visit. The shortest journey from Earth to Mars (when the two planets are closest to each other in their orbits) will take about six months. The first trip to Mars will be a long, dangerous, and expensive expedition.

An unmanned spacecraft full of supplies and tools, and designed to serve as a power-generating unit, will already have landed at the site two years earlier. The astronauts will need these facilities near their landing site in order to stay on Mars for eighteen months.[1]

The astronauts will feel very light on their feet when they take their first steps on the planet. Experiencing less gravity than on Earth, the astronauts will bounce around similar to the way the Apollo astronauts bounced as they walked on the Moon.

Their spacesuits will have to provide oxygen to breathe. The suits will also need to provide the pressure humans need to survive. The atmospheric pressure on the surface of Mars is equal to the atmospheric pressure at an altitude of 22 miles (35 kilometers) above Earth.[2]

The sky above these astronauts will usually be

If astronauts land on Mars in the future, they will need a place to live. This artist's idea of a completed outpost includes the crew's two-story lander habitat, inflatable laboratory, and rover.

cloudless. It will appear in varying shades of dull red and pink during the day. The Sun will appear only 44 percent as bright as it appears in Earth's sky. At night, the sky will be black, with no city lights of any kind to dim the brightness of the stars. The moons Phobos and Deimos will appear, but they are much too small to light up the sky, as Earth's Moon often does.

The ground beneath their feet will probably be brownish red, a result of the rusting process. Depending on where the astronauts land, rocks and boulders may be scattered everywhere. The landscape may be very flat, or a volcanic mountain may be rising in the distance. If they land near the Valles Marineris, they will have a chance to walk to the edge and look down into the deepest canyon known in the solar system.

The astronauts may have to bring all the water they will need for the visit. If water is discovered beneath the surface by earlier spacecraft, the astronauts will bring equipment to process the water for many uses.

"If water is available in substantial volumes," said NASA scientist Dr. Michael Malin, "it would make it easier for human crews to access and use it—for drinking, to create breathable air, and to extract oxygen and hydrogen for rocket fuel or to be stored for use in portable energy sources."[3]

The only water known for certain on the surface of Mars is the ice at the polar ice caps. The astronauts could land there and process the ice into usable water.

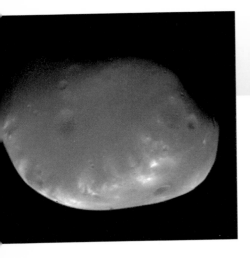

From the surface of Mars, the moon Deimos can be seen. But it is not bright enough to light up the night sky.

Mission planners may land future astronauts near one of the craters or canyons where probable sedimentary rock has been sighted. Once on the surface, astronauts may dig and drill into these rock layers. Later, they could analyze the rock samples with laboratory instruments in their spacecraft or habitat module. These astronauts may possibly find fossils of ancient life-forms in the deep layers of rock that have not been uncovered with robotic spacecraft.

Viewing Mars From Earth

Observing Mars from Earth may not be as exciting as a visit to the planet, but it is still a great way for you to study the Red Planet. Astronomy magazines, such as *Astronomy* and *Sky & Telescope*, as well as some newspapers and Internet sites, include charts that will show you where to look for Mars in the night sky. Once you know where to look, Mars is easy to spot. You will quickly see why it is called the Red Planet. Its redness is unmistakable.

Using binoculars will not change your view of Mars.

The planet is too small and too far away. The red dot will simply become a red blur. A good quality telescope is required to observe any surface features on Mars. Another important requirement is that Earth's atmosphere be very calm in order for the telescope to make out the light and dark areas of Mars, as well as its polar ice caps.[4]

Astronomy magazines and Internet sites will also tell whether Mars and Earth are close or far away from each other in their orbits. The closeness of the two planets in their orbits will greatly affect how large and bright Mars appears in the sky.[5]

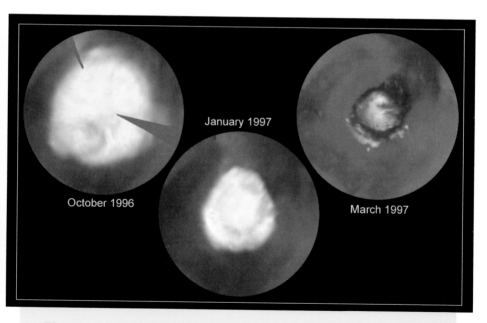

January 1997

October 1996

March 1997

This image of the north polar ice cap of Mars shows how the cap changes with the seasons. From Mars's spring in October 1996 to early summer in March 1997, the polar cap decreases in size.

If you do not have a telescope, ask at your school or local library whether your community has a local astronomy club. Members of astronomy clubs often give programs that allow the public to look through their telescopes. These programs are your chance to get a much closer look at Mars and other wonders in the universe.

Someday, you may be an explorer on Mars, and it may be you who uncovers evidence that life once existed on the Red Planet. If so, it would mean that life has existed on at least two of the planets in our solar system. Such a discovery would seem to increase the chances that many kinds of life exist on planets in other distant solar systems. So far, that discovery is only a possibility.

Until that day, scientists will continue their efforts to discover whether the ancient bringer of war may have once been a cradle of life. Such possibilities make the planet Mars a fascinating neighbor in space.

CHAPTER NOTES

Chapter 1. Martian Visitor

1. "Mars Pathfinder Concludes Primary Science Mission," *NASA Press Release, Jet Propulsion Laboratory*, August 8, 1997, <http://mars.jpl.nasa.gov/MPF/newspro/mpf/releases/pfprime/html> (April 6, 2001).

2. Jeff Schnauffer, "Drive, He Says," *People Weekly*, July 21, 1997, p. 55.

3. Ibid.

Chapter 2. Angry Red Planet

1. Bill Arnett, "Mars," *Nine Planets*, June 23, 2000, <http://www.seds.org/nineplanets/nineplanets/mars.html> (December 12, 2000).

2. Michael E. Bakich, *The Cambridge Planetary Handbook* (Cambridge, England: Cambridge University Press, 2000), pp. 178–180.

3. Ibid., pp. 182–185.

4. Arnett.

5. Dr. Michael A. Meyer, "Exobiology Strategy Report," *An Exobiological Strategy for Mars Exploration*, January 1995, <http://cmex-www.arc.nasa.gov/Exo_Strat/Docs/state.html> (December 12, 2000).

6. Jean Audouze and Guy Israel, *The Cambridge Atlas of Astronomy* (Cambridge, England: Cambridge University Press, 1996), p. 135.

7. Ibid., pp. 158–159.

8. Arnett.

9. Michael E. Bakich, *The Cambridge Planetary Handbook* (Cambridge, England: Cambridge University Press, 2000), pp. 165–202; Dr. David R. Williams, "Planetary Fact Sheet," *National Space Science Data Center Webpage*, January 18, 2001, <http://nssdc.gsfc.nasa.gov/planetary/factsheet/index.html> (April 6, 2001).

Chapter 3. Missions to Mars
1. J. Kelly Beatty, Carolyn Petersen, and Andrew Chaikin, eds., *The New Solar System* (Cambridge, England: Cambridge University Press, 1999), p. 150.
2. Ibid., pp. 149, 152.
3. Daniel S. Goldin, "Statement from Daniel S. Goldin, NASA Administrator," *NASA Press Releases 1996 Page*, August 6, 1996, <http://www.nasa.gov/releases/1996/> (December 6, 2000).
4. Michael E. Bakich, *The Cambridge Planetary Handbook* (Cambridge, England: Cambridge University Press, 2000), pp. 187–189.
5. Beatty, Petersen, and Chaikin, pp. 145–146.
6. Ibid., pp. 144–145.
7. Bakich, p. 193.
8. "Evidence of Martian Land of Lakes Discovered," *NASA Jet Propulsion Laboratory News Releases*, December 4, 2000, <http://www.jpl.nasa.gov> (December 8, 2000).
9. Ibid.
10. Dr. David R. Williams, "New Images Suggest Present-Day Sources of Liquid Water on Mars," *National Space Science Data Center Homepage*, NASA Goddard Space Flight Center, June 22, 2000, <http://nssdc.gsfc.nasa.gov/planetary/news/mars_water_pr_20000622.html> (April 6, 2001).
11. "High Resolution Images Show Big Differences Between Mars Polar Caps," *NASA Jet Propulsion Laboratory News Releases*, March 8, 2000, <http://mars.jpl.nasa.gov/msp98/news/news66.html> (April 6, 2001).

Chapter 4. Mars from Near and Far
1. Robert Zubrin, "The Mars Direct Plan," *Scientific American Webpage*, n.d., <http://www.sciam.com/2000/0300issue/0300zubrin.html> (April 6, 2001).
2. Michael E. Bakich, *The Cambridge Planetary Handbook* (Cambridge, England: Cambridge University Press, 2000), p. 192.
3. Dr. David R. Williams, "New Images Suggest Present-Day Sources of Liquid Water on Mars," *National Space Science Data Center Homepage*, NASA Goddard Space Flight Center, June 22, 2000, <http://nssdc.gsfc.nasa.gov/planetary/news/mars_water_pr_20000622.html> (April 6, 2001).
4. Rick Shaffer, *Your Guide to the Sky* (Chicago: Lowell House, 1999), pp. 82–85.
5. Ibid.

GLOSSARY

asteroids—Rocky bodies that orbit the Sun and range from boulder-sized to 600 miles wide. Most exist in the asteroid belt, an area between the orbits of Mars and Jupiter.

constellation—A pattern or arrangement of stars in the night sky. There are eighty-eight constellations recognized by professional astronomers.

core—The central interior of a planet or other body in space.

crater—The formation created by the impact of an object from space.

crust—The outermost layer of a planet's surface.

mantle—The inner layer of a planet that surrounds its core.

meteor—Rocky or icy material in space, from as small as a grain of sand to as big as a house, that enters Earth's atmosphere. Friction with air molecules in Earth's atmosphere causes the material to burn up, creating a streak of light, or "falling star," in the sky.

meteorite—A rock from space that has survived the trip through Earth's atmosphere and fallen to the ground on a planet or moon.

orbit—The path an object in space takes around another object in space because of gravitational attraction.

volcanoes—Vents in a planet's crust from which molten, or liquid, material from the interior is ejected.

FURTHER READING

Books

Cole, Michael D. *Living on Mars: Mission to the Red Planet.* Springfield, N.J.: Enslow Publishers, Inc., 1999.

Getz, David. *Life on Mars.* New York: Henry Holt & Co., Inc., 1997.

Raeburn, Paul. *Mars: Uncovering the Secrets of the Red Planet.* Washington, D.C.: National Geographic Society, 1998.

Skurzynski, Gloria. *Discover Mars.* Washington, D.C.: National Geographic Society, 1998.

Spangenburg, Ray, and Kit Moser. *A Look at Mars.* Danbury, Conn.: Franklin Watts, Inc., 2000.

Vogt, Gregory L. *The Solar System: Facts and Exploration.* New York: Twenty-First Century Books, 1995.

Internet Addresses

Lunar and Planetary Institute. *Exploring Mars.* n.d. <http://www.lpi.usra.edu/expmars/expmars.html>.

NASA/Ames Space Science Division. *Center for Mars Exploration Home Page.* n.d. <http://www.cmex.arc.nasa.gov/>.

NASA/Ames Space Science Division. *Mars Today.* n.d. <http://humbabe.arc.nasa.gov/MarsToday.html>.

NASA/2001 Mars Odyssesy. n.d. <http://mars.jpl.nasa.gov/odyssey/>.

Views of the Solar System. *Mars Introduction.* June 2000. <http://www.planetscapes.com/solar/eng/mars.htm>.

INDEX